IT'S TIME TO EAT AVOCADOS

It's Time to Eat Avocados

Walter the Educator

Silent King Books
A WhichHead Entertainment Imprint

Copyright © 2024 by Walter the Educator

All rights reserved. No part of this book may be reproduced in any manner whatsoever without written per- mission except in the case of brief quotations embodied in critical articles and reviews.

First Printing, 2024

Disclaimer

This book is a literary work; the story is not about specific persons, locations, situations, and/or circumstances unless mentioned in a historical context. Any resemblance to real persons, locations, situations, and/or circumstances is coincidental. This book is for entertainment and informational purposes only. The author and publisher offer this information without warranties expressed or implied. No matter the grounds, neither the author nor the publisher will be accountable for any losses, injuries, or other damages caused by the reader's use of this book. The use of this book acknowledges an understanding and acceptance of this disclaimer.

It's Time to Eat Avocados is a collectible early learning book by Walter the Educator suitable for all ages belonging to Walter the Educator's Time to Eat Book Series. Collect more books at WaltertheEducator.com

USE THE EXTRA SPACE TO TAKE NOTES AND DOCUMENT YOUR MEMORIES

AVOCADOS

It's time to eat avocados,

It's Time to Eat
Avocados

Soft and green and bright,

They're creamy on the inside,

And oh, what a delight!

From tree to plate, they travel,

With a bumpy, dark green skin,

But slice them up, and soon you'll see,

The treasure hid within.

With a twist and pop, the pit comes out,

It's big and round and smooth,

But it's the soft, green fruit around,

That's really made to soothe.

Spread it on some toast, so nice,

Or mash it in a bowl,

Add a pinch of salt or spice,

To make the flavors roll.

It's Time to Eat
Avocados

Dip it with some veggies,

Or spoon it up with care,

Avocados are so yummy,

You'll want to eat your share.

Full of vitamins and things,

That help us grow up strong,

Avocados are our tasty friends,

They help us all along.

For breakfast, lunch, or dinner,

Or snack time in between,

Avocados make us happy,

With their lovely shade of green.

So if you see that bumpy fruit,

Don't be shy or slow,

It's time to eat avocados

Just slice, and taste, and go!

Here's a little trick to try

Squeeze some lemon juice,

It keeps the green fresh, bright, and clear,

It's Time to Eat
Avocados

And adds a tangy boost!

So next time you're at snack time,

Or setting up your meal,

Remember that avocados

Are a creamy, dreamy deal!

ABOUT THE CREATOR

Walter the Educator is one of the pseudonyms for Walter Anderson. Formally educated in Chemistry, Business, and Education, he is an educator, an author, a diverse entrepreneur, and he is the son of a disabled war veteran. "Walter the Educator" shares his time between educating and creating. He holds interests and owns several creative projects that entertain, enlighten, enhance, and educate, hoping to inspire and motivate you. Follow, find new works, and stay up to date with Walter the Educator™

at WaltertheEducator.com

Milton Keynes UK
Ingram Content Group UK Ltd.
UKHW022051111124
451035UK00014B/1065